Nihongo: *Kana* —— An Introduction to the Japanese Syllabary

日本語
かな入門
英語版
新装版

JAPANFOUNDATION　国際交流基金日本語国際センター
THE JAPAN FOUNDATION JAPANESE-LANGUAGE INSTITUTE, URAWA

目　　次

まえがき
本書の使い方
※アクセントの記号について

ま　え　が　き

　本書は，主として海外において日本語を学習しようとする外国人を対象
として，「ひらがな」と「かたかな」を習得させる目的で作成したもので
ある。

　語例・文例は，できるだけ基礎的なものを選び，入門期の会話学習にも
役立つよう心がけるとともに，意味の理解を助け，学習効果を高める目的
でさし絵を入れた。また，正しく発音をしたり聞いたりするために，すべ
ての語にアクセントの記号をつけた。

Foreword

1. This textbook was prepared for the purpose of teaching *hiragana* and *katakana* to students in other countries who are learning Japanese as a foreign language.

2. Insofar as possible, the words and sentences selected have been limited to basic items that may also be used in teaching conversation during the introductory period. To further facilitate effective learning, the meanings of vocabulary items have been illustrated and accent lines have been placed above each word as an additional guide to correct hearing and pronunciation.

本書の使い方

本書の構成および使用法は次のとおりである。

第1部　ひらがな
1.　その課で練習するかながローマ字とともに示してある。

　　1字1字，教師の発音を聞いて，自分でも発音しながら，読み方と書き方を習得する。

　　1課から5課までは，練習の用紙がついているから，これによって，正しい字形・正しい書き順をしっかり身につけてほしい。

2.　次にその課で提出される字で表記できる単語があり，そのすべてにさし絵がついている。また，さし絵のほかに，脚注として，提出語のすべてに英訳がつけてある。

　　かなは1字だけで使われることは少ない。単語や文章，すなわち，いくつかの音のまとまりで使われる。いくつかの音のまとまりを文字化する練習をここで行う。

　　教師の発音どおりに自分でも発音しながら，ノートなど別の用紙を使って練習する。

3.　（れんしゅう）
　　覚えたかなを使って，別の単語を書くことにより，既習のかなの定着化をはかるものである。

　　ます目の中に書くようにしてあるのは，日本語の発音が1字1拍を原則としていることをしっかり覚えてもらいたいからである。

　　ここでも，左側に出ているかなを見て写すだけでなく，訳によってその単語の意味をつかみ，教師の発音を自分でもくり返しながら，音と文字と意味をむすびつけて覚えるようにしてほしい。

4. （かきとり）

　　左側にローマ字書きの単語がある。それをます目に書く練習である。

　　ローマ字表記は，国によって異なった発音をされてしまうことが多いので，使いたくないのだが，独習のばあいを考えて，あえてローマ字書き単語をつけた。

　　できれば，教師の発音を聞きながら書くようにしてほしい。

　　ここに取り上げた単語は，それまでに提出したものばかりなので，正答は自分でさがしてもらいたい。

　　また，ここは各自で配点を考え，テストとしてやってみることもできる。

　　なお，1課から6課までは，文字の数とます目の数は同じにしてあるが，7課からは，ます目の数を文字の数より多くしてある。学習者自身に字数を考えさせるためである。

　　外国人学習者にとっては，長音，とくにウ列・オ列の長音を聞きとることが困難なため，しばしば「う」を落としたり，つけすぎたりするようなことがある。このような点に注意を向けさせるために，ます目の数を文字より多くしたのである。

5. （テスト）

　　清音・濁音の提出された5課のうしろと，促音・拗音の提出された10課のうしろとに，テストを50題ずつつけた。これも，左側に問題がローマ字で書かれているが，できることなら，このローマ字書きの部分を何かでかくして見えないようにし，教師の発音をよく聞いて書きとるようにしてほしい。

6. （字形の似たひらがな）

　　3課に類似形のかなの表をつけた。左側に似た形の字をあげ，右側にその字を使った語をあげた。つまり，似た形をもつ語のペアである。この字や語をカードに写し，交互に見せて，似た字の識別練習を行う

こともできる。

第2部　かたかな
1.　かたかなについて
　　かたかなは次のばあいに用いられる。
　(1)外来語
　(2)外国の人名・地名，その他の固有名詞
　(3)動物・植物の名
　(4)擬声語（擬態語も，時によってかたかなで表記される場合がある）
　(5)とくに他と区別しようとする場合
　　　常用漢字外の漢字の使用を避けるばあい，ひらがなで書くと，ま
　　わりのひらがなの中に埋没してしまって，印象が薄れてしまうこと
　　がある。そんなときにはひらがな書きにせず，かたかなにすると，
　　漢字を使ったときよりも注意をひくという効果がある。
　(6)電報文

　　かたかなというと，一般に外来語を表記する文字という印象が強い
　が，上に述べたように，本来の日本語を表記することのほうが多いの
　である。

　　外来語といってもすでに日本語となっているもので，したがって発
　音も，日本語の音韻体系の中に組み入れられているものであることに
　注意してほしい。

　　「かたかな」は，付表の「かたかなの字源」に示したように，漢字
　の一部を取り出してつくられたものである。したがって，その多くは，
　そのまま漢字の「偏」や「旁」として通用するものである。だから，
　かたかなを書写練習するにあたって，漢字の初歩を勉強するつもりで，
　字形をしっかりと覚えこんでもらいたい。

2. かたかなの学習

本書では，次のように学習してほしい。

(1) 清音

かたかなの清音はひらがな清音46字と同じであるが，本書では，「ヲ」（ワ行のO）は除いてある。

この45字を一つの課に提出したが，これを三つぐらいに分け，少しずつ覚えるようにしてほしい。

練習用紙がついているから，そのます目いっぱいに，字形や書き順に注意しながら書いてもらいたい。

次に，ひらがなの学習に使った単語をかたかなにも使って，文字の定着につとめる。

(2) 濁音・拗音

清音と同様，ひらがな学習のときに使った単語・練習を使って，完全に覚えるようにすること。

(3) 外来語の表記のしかた

外国人学習者の困難点の一つは外来語の表記である。外国語の音にひかれてまちがえてしまったり，日本語にない音を日本語でどう表したらよいか迷ったりするからである。

本書では，外来語の表記でとくに誤りやすい長音・促音の書き方を中心に練習を作成してみた。

取り上げた単語の大部分は，外来語のほとんどが英語からきているため，英語からの語でしめられている。

本書に使われた単語は，すべて現代日本語として用いられている外来語である。しかし，「ウォッチ」のようにそれ自体としては「時計」という語が使われ，「ウォッチ」としては使われないが，「ストップ・ウォッチ」のような複合語として表現される語も含まれている。

※ アクセントの記号について

　アクセントの表記は，「明解日本語アクセント辞典」（三省堂・昭和48年）および「日本語発音アクセント辞典」（日本放送協会・昭和41年）の表記にしたがった。

　日本語のアクセントは強弱アクセントではなく高低アクセントである。

　アクセントは語の上部に「－」「┐」の印をつけ，「アイ」「ウオ」のように示した。「－」は，その部分の拍を高く発音し，「┐」は，その部分が高く，次の拍から低くなることを示す。

　共通語としてのアクセントは次の4種である。

a）（例）　　う̲し（牛）　　　　→　　う̲し（が）
　　　　　　す̲いか（西瓜）　　→　　す̲いか（が）
　　　　　　ち̲かてつ（地下鉄）→　　ち̲かてつ（が）

　　語の第1拍のみ低く，第2拍目からあとの拍はすべて高く発音するもの。その語に助詞「が」などをつけて発音するばあいにもそのまま高く発音する。

b）（例）　　な̲つ（夏）　　　　→　　な̲つ（が）
　　　　　　あ̲たま（頭）　　　→　　あ̲たま（が）

　　語の第1拍を低く，第2拍目から語の最後の拍まで高く発音し，その語に助詞「が」などがついたばあいには，助詞の部分を低く発音する。

c）（例）　　こ̲こ̲ろ（心）
　　　　　　く̲だ̲もの（果物）
　　　　　　お̲と̲とい（一昨日）

　　語の第1拍を低く，中間の拍を高く，その後の拍をまた低く発音する。

d）（例）　　ご̲ご（午後）
　　　　　　き̲んこ（金庫）
　　　　　　ろ̲っぷん（六分）

　　語の第1拍のみを高く，それに続くあとの拍はすべて低く発音する。

Description of the Text and Recommendations for its Effective Utilization

Part I *Hiragana*

1. At the beginning of each lesson, the *kana* to be practiced are presented together with their romanization. The student should first listen to the sound of each *kana* as it is pronounced by the teacher. Then, while pronouncing it himself, the student should learn to read and write it. Lessons 1 ~ 5 include a practice page, which the learner should use to master the form and stroke order of each *kana* character.

2. Next comes a list of words which can be written using the *kana* introduced in the current and previous lessons. Each of these words has been illustrated in the text and translated into English in the footnotes.

   A single *kana* is rarely used alone; *kana* are used in words and sentences, i.e. within units consisting of a number of sounds. Hence practice in writing such multi-sound units is given here. These words should be practiced by writing them while simultaneously pronouncing them in the same way as the teacher.

3. (Practice)

   Assimilation of the *kana* being taught is achieved through practice in writing additional words. Boxes have been provided for writing practice in order to emphasize that one *kana* represents one mora. This should not be simply an exercise in copying the *kana* given on the left. Rather, here too, each word should be learned as an association of sound, *kana* and meaning by first understanding it through translation and then repeating the pronunciation of the teacher.

4. (Dictation)

The dictation exercise provides practice in transliterating the romanized words given on the left side of the page into *hiragana.* Because the pronunciation of Roman letters varies from country to country, their use is undesirable in this exercise; romanized words have been included here as an aid for the independent learners.

If at all possible, the dictation exercise should be written while listening to the pronunciation of the tape or teacher.

Since the vocabulary items used in this exercise have been selected from those already presented, the student should be encouraged to find the answers himself. This can also be used as a self-graded test.

From lessons 1 ∼ 6, the number of boxes corresponds to the number of *kana*; after lesson 6, the number of boxes has been increased so as to force the student to judge the number necessary. Foreign learners have difficulty hearing the long sounds of Japanese, especially those containing *u* and *o*; *u* is frequently dropped or added incorrectly. The number of boxes has been increased to draw attention to this point.

5. (Test)

Two tests of fifty problems each have been included following lessons 5 and 10. Here, too, the problems have been given in *romaji,* but if possible, this *romaji* should be covered and the test be written while listening to the teacher.

6. (*Hiragana* having similar forms)

Kana having similar shapes have been listed in a chart, *kana* to the left and words using them to the right. In other words, these are pairs of words which have similar forms. The *kana* and words may be copied onto flash cards to use for practice in distinguishing similar *kana*.

Part II *Katakana*

1. About *katakana*

   Katakana is used for the following:

   (1) words of foreign origin

   (2) foreign personal names, place names and other proper nouns

   (3) names of plants and animals

   (4) onomatopoeia (and sometimes mimesis)

   (5) emphasis of a particular word

   Words written with Chinese characters that are no longer included in the *jōyō kanji* are now frequently written in *kana*. However, when written in *hiragana*, such words tend to be overwhelmed by the *hiragana* surrounding them and to lose their impact. Thus they are written in *katakana*, which has the effect of drawing more attention to them than if they were written in *kanji*.

   (6) telegrams

It should be obvious from this that *katakana*, which is generally thought of as being used to express words of foreign origin, is, in fact, more frequently used for words which are originally Japanese.

"Words of foreign origin", of course, refers to words which have already become Japanese, i.e. have been transformed to fit into the Japanese sound system.

Special note should be made of the origins of *katakana*, which were created by isolating elements of certain *kanji*. (Refer to Chart 2, "The Derivations of *Katakana*", p. 88.) In many cases, these elements are widely used as the radicals of *kanji*. When writing these *katakana*, the student should practice with the intention of taking a first step in the study of *kanji*, taking special care to learn the forms thoroughly.

2. Studying *katakana*

    This text should be studied in the following manner.

(1) *SEION* ーア・イ・ウ・エ・オ……ワ・ンー (Unmodified *kana*)

    The sounds represented by *katakana* are the same as those repre-
    sented by the 46 *hiragana*, however in this text ヲ (wo) has been
    omitted. All 45 *katakana* have been presented in one lesson, but they
    should be divided into three or so groups and learned a few at a time.
    Careful attention should be paid to the form and stroke order of the
    katakana, which the student should practice using the paper which
    has been included for that purpose.

    Next, the words which were used in learning *hiragana* should be
    written in *katakana* until the characters are mastered.

(2) *DAKUON* ーガ・ギ・グ・ゲ・ゴ etc. *YŌ-ON* ーキャ・キュ・キョ etc.
    (Modified *kana*)

    These should also be mastered by means of the words and methods
    employed in learning *hiragana*.

(3) Writing Words of Foreign Origin

    One problem for foreign learners is the writing of words of foreign
    origin. Students may, on the one hand, be drawn into too close an
    approximation of the word's original pronunciation or, on the other
    hand, may be uncertain as to how to express in *kana* a sound which
    does not exist in Japanese.

    The writing of words of foreign origin has been limited so as to focus on the major problems of foreign learners, namely, long vowel sounds and double consonant sounds. Since the majority of foreign words in Japanese have come from English, most of the examples given are English.

All the words of foreign origin appearing in this text are words used in modern Japanese. However, some words are included which, like *uottchi* (watch) are not used in their own right (*tokei* is used in this meaning) but do occur in compounds, such as *sutoppu-uottchi* (stop watch).

※　Accent Marks Used in This Book

Accent marks used in the book conform to the system used in *Meikai Nihongo Akusento Jiten* (Sanseido, 1973) and *Nihongo Hatsuon Akusento Jiten* (Nihon Hoso Kyokai, 1967).

The accent of Japanese is an accent of pitch rather than one of stress.

Pitch has been indicated by a line, '‾‾' or '‾‾' placed above a word, as for example: *āi, uō.* '‾‾' indicates that the mora(s) of this part of the word have high pitch; '‾‾' indicates that this part is given high pitch but that low pitch is to be used beginning with the next mora. In standard Japanese four accent patterns exist:

a) Examples:

ushi	(cow, ox)	→	ushi (ga)
suika	(watermelon)	→	suika (ga)
chikatetsu	(subway)	→	chikatetsu (ga)

Only the first mora of a word is low; from the second mora, all moras are spoken with a high pitch. When a particle such as *ga* is added to the word, this particle is also given high pitch.

b) Examples:

natsu' (summer)		→	natsu' (ga)
atama' (head)		→	atama' (ga)

The first mora is low and all following moras are high, but when a particle such as *ga* is added, the particle is spoken with low pitch.

c) Examples:

kokoro   (heart)

kudamono   (fruit)

ototoi   (the day before yesterday)

The first mora is spoken with low pitch, intervening moras with high pitch, and ensuing moras with low pitch.

d) Examples:

gogo   (afternoon)

kinko   (safe)

roppun   (six minutes)

Only the first mora is spoken with high pitch; all ensuing moras have low pitch.

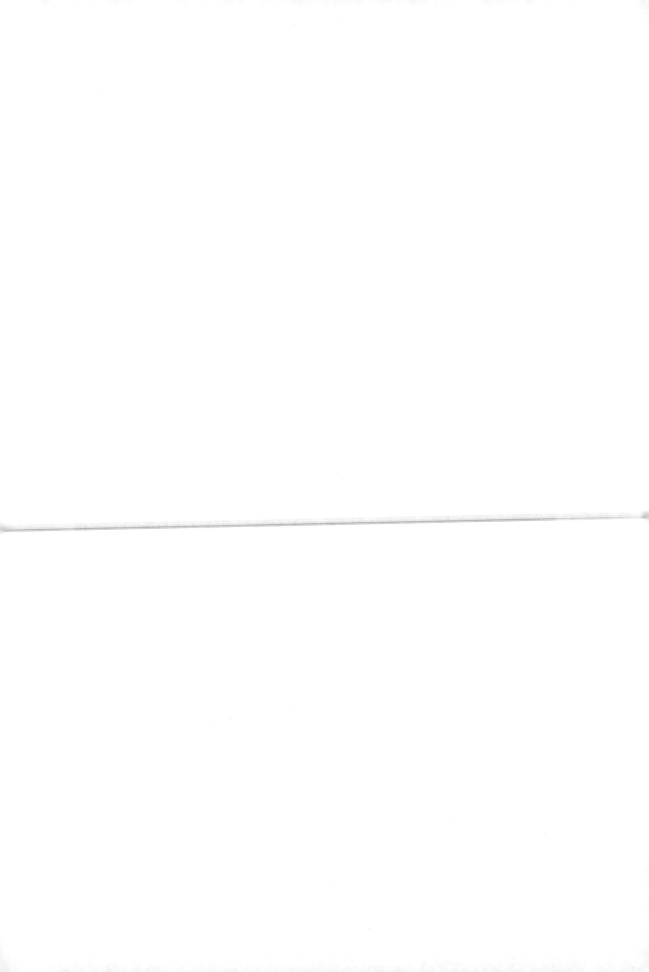

第1部　chart 1

ひ　ら　が　な

1課　あ行　か行　さ行

2課　た行　な行　は行

3課　ま行　や行　ら行　わ　を　ん

4課　が行　ざ行

5課　だ行　ば行　ぱ行

──テスト1

6課　□っか　□っさ　□った　□っぱ

7課　かあ　きい　くう　けい　こう

8課　きゃ　しゃ

9課　ちゃ　にゃ　ひゃ　みゃ　りゃ

10課　わたしは　ほんやへ　いきます

──テスト2

付表1　ひらがなの字源
　　　　The derivations of Hiragana

1 課

あ a　い i　う u　え e　お o
か ka　き ki　く ku　け ke　こ ko
さ sa　し shi　す su　せ se　そ so

あ　し
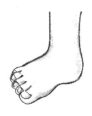

え　き

か　い

し　お

う　し

か　さ

あし foot　　かい shell　　うし cow, ox　　えき station
しお salt　　かさ umbrella

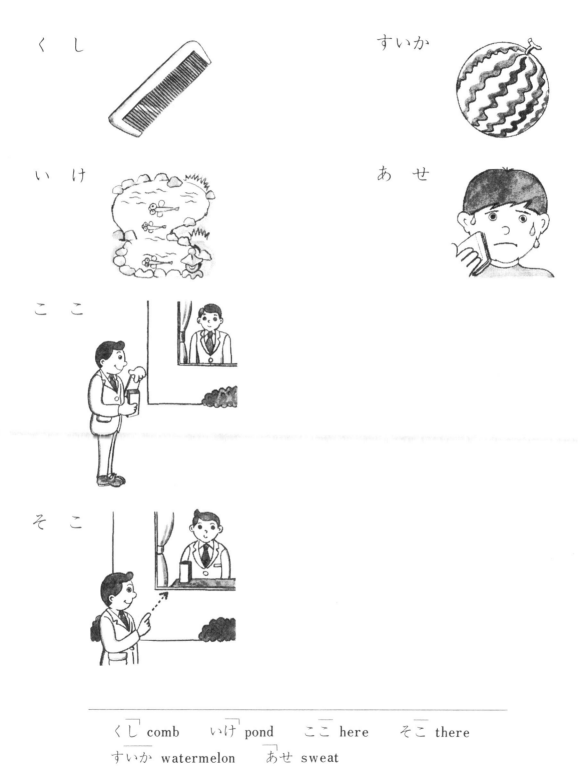

くし

すいか

いけ

あせ

ここ

そこ

くし comb　いけ pond　ここ here　そこ there
すいか watermelon　あせ sweat

ひらがな　あいうえおかきくけこさしすせそ　書き方練習

あ	い	う	え	お	か	き	く	け	こ	さ	し	す	せ	そ

（書き順・なぞり書き練習シート）

※「き」「さ」「そ」というかきかたもある。

き・さ・そ can also be written き・さ・そ.

〔れんしゅう〕

あかい	red			
あう	to meet			
え	picture			
あおい	blue			
さか	slope			
あき	autumn			
しかく	square			
さけ	sake			
いす	chair			
せかい	world			
きそく	regulation			
うそ	lie			

〔かきとり〕

1. ashi
2. kasa
3. suika
4. uso
5. eki
6. soko
7. sekai
8. kushi
9. shio
10. koko
11. kisoku
12. kai
13. ase
14. isu
15. shikaku

2 課

た ta　ち chi　つ tsu　て te　と to
な na　に ni　ぬ nu　ね ne　の no
は ha　ひ hi　ふ fu　へ he　ほ ho

たいこ

て

うち

いと

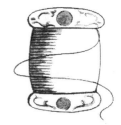

くつ

さかな

たいこ drum　　うち house　　くつ shoes　　て hand
いと thread　　さかな fish

＊「か・き・く・け・こ・さ・し・す・せ・そ・た・ち・つ・て・と・は・ひ・ふ・へ・ほ」
の前の「き」「く」「し」「す」「ち」「つ」「ひ」「ふ」は母音が無音化する。例：くつ kutsu.
The vowel sounds of ki, ku, shi, su, chi, tsu, hi and fu are unvoiced when they come
before ka, ki, ku, ke, ko, sa, shi, su, se, so, ta, chi, tsu, te, to, ha, hi, fu, he and ho;
for example: kutsu.

かに crab　　いぬ dog　　ねこ cat　　つの horn　　はし bridge
ひ fire　　ふえ flute　　へい wall　　ほし star

＊「へい」の発音は、人によって［hee］のように発音することがある。
Hei is pronounced ［hee］ by some native speakers.

たちつてとなにぬねのはひふへほ

〔れんしゅう〕

あした	tomorrow	
くち	mouth	
きせつ	season	
ちかてつ	subway	
おととい	the day before yesterday	
なつ	summer	
くに	country	
おかね	money	
はた	flag	
ふね	ship	
はな	flower	
ほね	bone	

〔かきとり〕

1. taiko　　　2. kuchi　　　3. sakana

4. chikatetsu　　　5. ototoi　　　6. kani

7. inu　　　8. tsuno　　　9. natsu

10. fune　　　11. hei　　　12. hoshi

13. hata　　　14. kutsu　　　15. okane

3 課

ま ma　み mi　む mu　め me　も mo
や ya　　　ゆ yu　　　よ yo
ら ra　り ri　る ru　れ re　ろ ro
わ wa　　　　　　を o　ん n

うま　　
みみ
むし
め
くも
やま

うま horse　みみ ear　むし insect　め eye　くも cloud
やま mountain

— 11 —

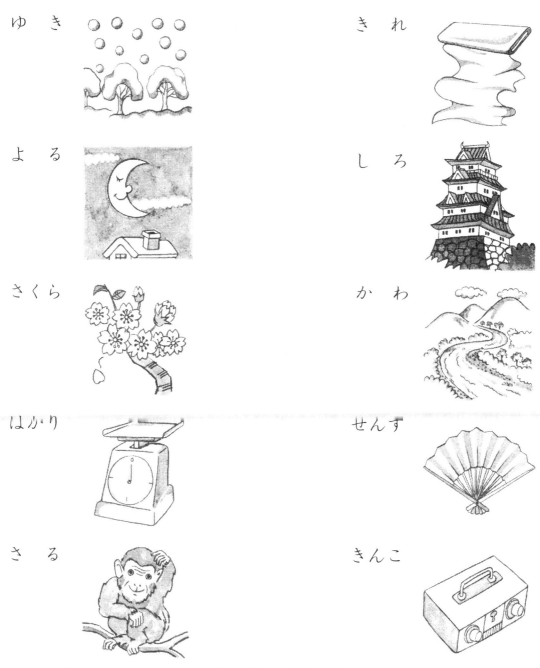

ゆき snow　よる night　さくら cherry blossoms　はかり scale
さる monkey　きれ cloth　しろ castle　かわ river　せんす folding fan
きんこ safe

＊「を」は助詞にしか使わない。
　　を is used only as a particle.

ま	ま	ま	ま	ま				
み	みみ	み	み	み				
む	むむ	む	む	む				
め	め	め	め	め				
も	もも	も	も	も				
や	つや	や	や	や				
ゆ	ゆゆ	ゆ	ゆ	ゆ				
よ	よよ	よ	よ	よ				
ら	らら	ら	ら	ら				
り	り	り	り	り				
る	る	る	る	る				
れ	れ	れ	れ	れ				
ろ	ろ	ろ	ろ	ろ				
わ	わ	わ	わ	わ				
を	をを	を	を	を				
ん	ん	ん	ん	ん				

※「や」「ゆ」というかきかたもある。
や・ゆ can also be written や・ゆ.

〔れんしゅう〕

あたま	head										
うみ	sea										
あめ	rain										
かいもの	shopping										
ゆめ	dream										
まくら	pillow										
おつり	change										
こころ	heart										
わたし	I										
にわ	garden										
らいねん	next year										
ほんや	book store										

〔かきとり〕

1. umi ☐☐   2. atama ☐☐☐   3. mushi ☐☐

4. me ☐   5. kumo ☐☐   6. yama ☐☐   7. yume ☐☐

8. yoru ☐☐   9. hon-ya ☐☐☐   10. watashi ☐☐☐

11. sakura ☐☐☐   12. otsuri ☐☐☐   13. kokoro ☐☐☐

14. sensu ☐☐☐   15. kire ☐☐

字形の似たひらがな　Hiragana Having Similar Forms

く ku ── へ he
- { く　くい（杭）　stake
- へ　へい（塀）　wall

す su ── ち chi
- { す　うす（臼）　mortar
- ち　うち（家）　house

り ri ── い i ── こ ko ── に ni
- { り　くり（栗）　chestnut
- い　くい（杭）　stake
- { こ　こい（鯉）　carp
- に　にい（二位）　second place

き ki ── さ sa ── た ta ── な na
- { き　えき（駅）　station
- さ　えさ（餌）　feed
- { た　かた（肩）　shoulder
- な　かな（仮名）　kana

は ha ── ほ ho ── ま ma ── も mo
│
よ yo
- { は　はし（橋）　bridge
- ほ　ほし（星）　star
- { ま　まり（毬）　ball
- も　もり（森）　woods

る ru ── ろ ro
- { る　くる（来る）　to come
- ろ　くろ（黒）　black

あ a ── め me ── ぬ nu
- { あ　あし（足）　foot
- め　めし（飯）　cooked rice

ぬ nu ── ね ne ── わ wa ── れ re
- { ね　かね（金）　metal, money
- わ　かわ（川）　river
- れ　かれ（彼）　he

4 課

が ga	ぎ gi	ぐ gu	げ ge	ご go
(が ŋa	ぎ ŋi	ぐ ŋu	げ ŋe	ご ŋo)
ざ za	じ ji	ず zu	ぜ ze	ぞ zo

がか

かぎ

めがね

ぐんじん
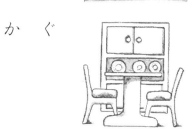

ぎんか

かぐ

がか painter　めがね spectacles　ぎんか silver coin　かぎ key
ぐんじん soldier　かぐ furniture

げ　た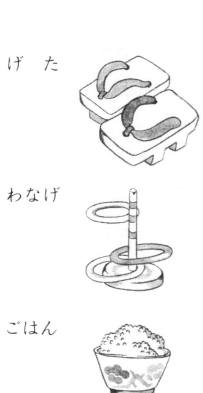

わなげ

ごはん

りんご

はいざら

ふじさん

ち　ず

か　ぜ

すいぞく
かん

げた wooden clogs　　わなげ quoits　　ごはん rice　　りんご apple　　はいざら ash tray

ふじさん Mt. Fuji　　　ちず map　　　かぜ wind　　　すいぞくかん aquarium

*が・ぎ・ぐ・げ・ご が，語の２拍以降にあらわれると，[ŋa]・[ŋi]・[ŋu]・[ŋe]・[ŋo]と発音される。

　Ga, gi, gu, ge and go are pronounced [ŋa], [ŋi], [ŋu], [ŋe] and [ŋo] except
　when they appear in the first syllable of a word.

が	が	が	が					
ぎ	ぎ	ぎ	ぎ					
ぐ	ぐ	ぐ	ぐ					
げ	げ	げ	げ					
ご	ご	ご	ご					
ざ	ざ	ざ	ざ					
じ	じ	じ	じ					
ず	ず	ず	ず					
ぜ	ぜ	ぜ	ぜ					
ぞ	ぞ	ぞ	ぞ					

〔れんしゅう〕

がいこくじん	foreigner	

がいこくじん foreigner

かがく chemistry

ぎんこう bank

みぎ right

めぐすり eye lotion

げんいん cause

ひげ beard

ごご P.M. afternoon

かざん volcano

みず water

ごぜん A.M. morning

かぞく family

〔かきとり〕

1. gaka

2. gozen

3. gogo

4. migi

5. kazoku

6. haizara

7. Fujisan

8. megane

9. kaze

10. gunjin

11. kagu

12. gen-in

13. suizokukan

14. wanage

15. ringo

5　課

だda　ぢji　づzu　でde　どdo

ばba　びbi　ぶbu　べbe　ぼbo

ぱpa　ぴpi　ぷpu　ぺpe　ぽpo

くだもの

かばん

でんわ

えび

まど

しんぶん

くだもの fruit　　でんわ telephone　　まど window　　かばん bag
えび shrimp　　しんぶん newspaper

かべ

おぼん

でんぱ

えんぴつ

てんぷら

さんぽ

かべ wall of house   おぼん tray   でんぱ radio wave

えんぴつ pencil   てんぷら tempura   さんぽ walk

＊「ん」も1拍と数える。だから，「さんぽ」は3拍である。

Syllabic n(ん) is counted as one mora. Hence sampo consists of three moras.

＊ji・zu は，じ・ず と書くことが原則であるが，はなぢ（はな＋ち）・みかづき（みか ＋つき）のように，ち・つを語頭にもつ語の連濁や，つづく・ちぢむのように，同音 の連呼による場合は，ぢ・づと書く。

Ji and zu are written じ and ず except in the following situations, where ぢ and づ are used: 1) when a word beginning with chi or tsu follows another element in a compound word, such as はなぢ (nose bleed) 〔hanaji＝はな＋ち〕or みかづ き (new moon) 〔mikazuki＝みか＋つき〕; 2) when the same sound occurs twice in succession, such as つづく (continue) tsuzuku or ちぢむ (shrink) chijimu.

だ	だ	だ	だ					
ぢ	ぢ	ぢ	ぢ					
づ	づ	づ	づ					
で	で	で	で					
ど	ど	ど	ど					
ば	ば	ば	ば					
び	び	び	び					
ぶ	ぶ	ぶ	ぶ					
べ	べ	べ	べ					
ぼ	ぼ	ぼ	ぼ					
ぱ	ぱ	ぱ	ぱ					
ぴ	ぴ	ぴ	ぴ					
ぷ	ぷ	ぷ	ぷ					
ぺ	ぺ	ぺ	ぺ					
ぽ	ぽ	ぽ	ぽ					

〔れんしゅう〕

ひだり	left	
えだ	branch	
うで	arm	
でんき	electricity	
おどり	dance	
こども	child	
たばこ	cigarette	
ゆび	finger	
へび	snake	
ぶんか	culture	
なべ	pan	
ぼいん	vowel	

〔かきとり〕

1. kudamono
2. denwa
3. mado
4. denki
5. empitsu
6. shimbun
7. kaban
8. tabako
9. nabe
10. hebi
11. odori
12. boin
13. kodomo
14. yubi
15. bunka

テスト　1

　テープを聞いて，下の ☐☐☐ の中に，ひらがなを書き入れなさい。

1．uta ☐☐

2．natsu ☐☐

3．kasa ☐☐

4．uso ☐☐

5．inu ☐☐

6．neko ☐☐

7．saru ☐☐

8．fune ☐☐

9．mame ☐☐

10．fue ☐☐

11．yoru ☐☐

12．yuki ☐☐

13．yane ☐☐

14．heya ☐☐

15．yume ☐☐

16 . kisoku ⬚⬚⬚

17 . sekai ⬚⬚⬚

18 . tsukue ⬚⬚⬚

19 . ototoi ⬚⬚⬚⬚

20 . sensu ⬚⬚⬚

21 . kinko ⬚⬚⬚

22 . rainen ⬚⬚⬚⬚

23 . hon-ya ⬚⬚⬚

24 . kamisori ⬚⬚⬚⬚

25 . sakana ⬚⬚⬚

26 . hakari ⬚⬚⬚

27 . otsuri ⬚⬚⬚

28 . kazoku ⬚⬚⬚

29 . kazan ⬚⬚⬚

30 . haizara ⬚⬚⬚⬚

31 . suki ⬚⬚

32 . tsuki ⬚⬚

33 . tsuna ⬚⬚

34 . suna ⬚⬚

35 . chika ⬚⬚

36 . shika ⬚⬚

37 . kata ⬚⬚

38 . hata ⬚⬚

39 . kana ⬚⬚

40 . kan-na ⬚⬚⬚

41 . kuchi ⬚⬚

42. kushi ☐☐

43. uchi ☐☐

44. ushi ☐☐

45. kin ☐☐

46. gin ☐☐

47. kagi ☐☐

48. kani ☐☐

49. kami ☐☐

50. kaki ☐☐

6 課

促音は，小さな「っ」で表す。「っ」も1拍の長さで発音しなければならない。

Double consonant sounds are indicated by a small 〔っ〕 preceding the <u>kana</u> containing the consonant sound. This 〔っ〕 means that the following consonant is to be given two syllables' duration.

□っか―kka	□っき―kki	□っく―kku	□っけ―kke	□っこ―kko
□っさ―ssa	□っし―sshi	□っす―ssu	□っせ―sse	□っそ―sso
□った―tta	□っち―tchi	□っつ―ttsu	□って―tte	□っと―tto
□っぱ―ppa	□っぴ―ppi	□っぷ―ppu	□っぺ―ppe	□っぽ―ppo

らっかさん

せっけん

がっき

けっこん

らっかさん parachute　　がっき musical instrument

せっけん soap　　けっこん marriage

ざっし

きって

らっぱ

きっぷ

ほっぺた

ざっし magazine　　きって stamp　　らっぱ bugle, trumpet
きっぷ ticket　　ほっぺた cheek

〔れんしゅう〕

いっかい　first floor

さっか　writer

にっき　diary

はっけん　discovery

いっさつ　one book

はっせん　eight thousand

けっせき　absence

ほっぺた　cheek

ねったい　the tropics

あさって　the day after tomorrow

こぎって　cheque

いっぷん　one minute

ろっぷん　six minutes

しっぱい　failure

せいねんがっぴ　date of birth

〔かきとり〕

1. rakkasan
2. gakki
3. ikkai
4. sakka
5. nikki
6. sekken
7. hakken
8. kekkon
9. issatsu
10. zasshi
11. hassen

12. kesseki
13. nettai
14. kitte
15. asatte
16. kogitte
17. rappa
18. kippu
19. ippun
20. roppun
21. shippai
22. hoppeta

7 課

かあ kaa(kā)　さあ saa(sā)　たあ taa(tā)

きい kii(kī)　しい shii(shī)　ちい chii(chī)

くう kuu(kū)　すう suu(sū)　つう tsuu(tsū)

けい kei(kē)　せい sei(sē)　てい tei(tē)　ねえ nee(nē)

こう koo(kō)　そう soo(sō)　とう too(tō)　おお oo(ō)　とお too(tō)

おかあさん

おにいさん

おばあさん

せんぷうき

おじいさん

ふうとう

おかあさん mother　おばあさん grandmother　おじいさん grandfather

おにいさん elder brother　せんぷうき electric fan　ふうとう envelope

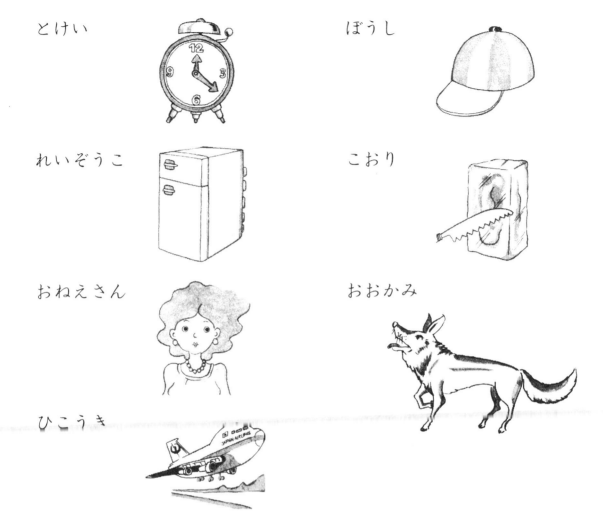

とけい

ぼうし

れいぞうこ

こおり

おねえさん

おおかみ

ひこうき

とけい watch, clock　　れいぞうこ refrigerator　　おねえさん elder sister

ひこうき airplane　　ぼうし hat, cap　　こおり ice　　おおかみ wolf

＊お列長音で「—お」と書くものは，あまり多くない。次の語は「—お」と書くことに
なっている。
　　おおい，おおやけ，おおきい，こおり，とおい，こおる，とおる，こおろぎ など。
　　Although they are few, there are some words in which long —o is written with
　　—お, such as the following: おおい (many), おおやけ (public), おおきい (big),
　　こおり (ice), とおい (far), とおる (pass), こおろぎ (cricket), etc.

〔れんしゅう〕

えいご　　English

けいざい　　economy

がくせい　　student

へいわ　　peace

めいし　　noun

くうき　　air

こうつう　　transportation

つうしん　　correspondence

ばんごう　　number

ぞう　　elephant

ぼうえき　　foreign trade

ぶんぽう　　grammar

げつようび　Monday

とおか　the 10th
ten days

おおきい　big, large

とおい　far

〔かきとり〕

1. okaasan

2. obaasan

3. eigo

4. keizai

5. ojiisan

6. oniisan

7. gakusei

8. heiwa

9. tokei

10. oneesan

11. kootsuu

12. bangoo

13. hikooki

14. bumpoo

15. booeki

16. tsuushin

17. zoo

18. koori

19. ookii

20. tooka

8 課

き ゃ kya	き ゅ kyu	き ょ kyo
ぎ ゃ gya	ぎ ゅ gyu	ぎ ょ gyo
し ゃ sha	し ゅ shu	し ょ sho
じ ゃ ja	じ ゅ ju	じ ょ jo

きゃく

けんびきょう
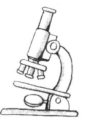

ちきゅう

きんぎょ

すいぎゅう

にんぎょう

きゃく guest　　ちきゅう earth　　すいぎゅう water buffalo
けんびきょう microscope　　きんぎょ goldfish　　にんぎょう doll

いしゃ

じゅうどう

じてんしゃ

はつでんしょ

じんじゃ

しょうぼう
じどうしゃ

いしゃ doctor　　じてんしゃ bicycle　　じんじゃ Shinto shrine

じゅうどう judo　　はつでんしょ power station

しょうぼうじどうしゃ fire engine

〔れんしゅう〕

きゅうきゅうしゃ
　　　　ambulance

げっきゅう　　monthly salary

きょねん　　　last year

べんきょう　　study

ゆうびんきょく
　　　　post office

こうぎょう　　industry

のうぎょう　　agriculture

かいしゃ　　　　company

うんてんしゅ　driver

じゅうにがつ　December

じゅうしょ　　address

びじゅつかん　art museum

じしょ　　　　dictionary

しょうがくきん

　　　　　　scholarship

こうじょう　　factory

〔かきとり〕

1．kyaku

2．chikyuu

3．gekkyuu

4．kyonen

5．suigyuu

6．benkyoo

7．kembikyoo

8．kingyo

9．noogyoo

10．ningyoo

11．koogyoo

12．juusho

13．jisho

14．koojoo

15．juudoo

16．hatsudensho

17．jitensha

18．isha

19．juunigatsu

20．untenshu

9 課

ちゃ cha	ちゅ chu	ちょ cho
にゃ nya	にゅ nyu	にょ nyo
ひゃ hya	ひゅ hyu	ひょ hyo
びゃ bya	びゅ byu	びょ byo
ぴゃ pya	ぴゅ pyu	ぴょ pyo
みゃ mya	みゅ myu	みょ myo
りゃ rya	りゅ ryu	りょ ryo

こうちゃ

ちゅうしゃ

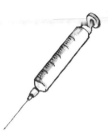

かぼちゃ

ちょっかく

こうちゃ black tea　　かぼちゃ squash　　ちゅうしゃ injection
ちょっかく right angle

ちょうちん

びょういん

ぎゅうにゅう

みゃく

ひゃくえん

りょこう

ひょうざん

りゅう

ちょうちん paper lantern　ぎゅうにゅう milk　ひゃくえん one hundred yen

ひょうざん ice berg　びょういん hospital　みゃく pulse

りょこう trip, travel　りゅう dragon

「ちゃ」は1拍で発音するが，表記の場合は，「ち」「ゃ」と2字で表す。この「や」「ゆ」「よ」は，下のように小さく書く。

ちゃ is pronounced as one mora although it is written with two <u>kana</u>, ち and や. In such cases, や, ゆ and よ are written small in the manner shown below:

よこ書きの場合は，左の例のように「や」「ゆ」「よ」をますの左下に小さく書く。

When writing horizontally, や, ゆ and よ are written small in the lower lefthand part of the square.

たて書きの場合は，左の例のように「や」「ゆ」「よ」をますの右上に小さく書く。

When writing vertically, や, ゆ and よ are written small in the upper righthand part of the square.

[れんしゅう]

うちゅう
universe

ちゅうがっこう
junior high school

こうちょう
principal, headmaster

ゆにゅう
import

にひゃく
two hundred

さんびゃく
three hundred

はっぴゃく
eight hundred

いちびょう
one second

びょうき
illness

みょうじ
family name

りょうしゅうしょ
receipt

りゅうがくせい
foreign student

だいとうりょう
president
(of a country)

〔かきとり〕

1. koocha
2. uchuu
3. chuugakkoo
4. chuusha
5. chokkaku
6. choochin
7. yu-nyuu

8. gyuu-nyuu

9. sambyaku

10. nihyaku

11. roppyaku

12. byooin

13. myaku

14. byooki

15. myooji

16. ryokoo

17. ryuu

18. ryooshuusho

19. daitooryoo

20. ryuugakusei

10 課

助詞のwaは「は」，e は「へ」，o は「を」と書く。

The particle <u>wa</u> is written as は, <u>e</u> as へ and <u>o</u> as を.

こんにちは。(1)

わたしは　たなかです。(2)

それは　なんですか。(3)

これは　わたしの　かばんです。(4)

どこへ　いきますか。(5)

ほんやへ　いきます。(6)

ほんやで　なにを　かいますか。(7)

ざっしと　じしょを　かいます。(8)

それから，きっさてんへ　いって，こうちゃを　のみます。(9)

---

(1) Hello.
(2) I'm Tanaka.
(3) What is that?
(4) This is my bag.
(5) Where are you going?
(6) I'm going to the book store.

(7) What are you going to buy at the book store?
(8) I'm going to buy a magazine and a dictionary.
(9) After that, I'll go to a coffee shop and drink some tea.

〔れんしゅう〕

kombanwa (1)

ohayoo gozaimasu (2)

sayoonara (3)

kore wa tsukue desu (4)

doko e ikimasu ka? (5)

---

(1) Good evening.

(2) Good morning.

(3) Good-bye.

(4) This is a desk.

(5) Where are you going?

ginkoo e ikimasu (6)

shimbun o totte
kudasai (7)

arigatoo gozaimasu (8)

ocha o nomimasu (9)

---

(6) I'm going to the bank.

(7) Please get me the newspaper.

(8) Thank you.

(9) I'm going to drink some tea.

テスト　2

テープを聞いて □□□□□ の中にひらがなを書き入れなさい。

1. kekka

2. hatsuon

3. nettai

4. atsui

5. shippai

6. zasshi

7. kekkon

8. kitte

9. rokusatsu

10. kesseki

11. rokusen-en

12. gakki

13. kippu

14. asatte

15. rokuon

16. satoo

17. mado

18 . undoo

19 . bangoo

20 . booeki

21 . sekidoo

22 . booshi

23 . yoochi-en

24 . tenkiyohoo

25 . reizooko

26 . keisatsu

27 . ondo

28 . kinoo

29 . bumpoo

30 . kootsuu

31 . ningyo

32 . kin-jo

33 . toshokan

34 . noogyoo

35 . jisho

36 . kashu

37 . gyuuniku

38 . kembikyoo

39 . gekkyuu

40 . kyuukoo

41 . kingyo

42 . kyonen

43 . shokudoo

44 . shooyu

45 . juusho

46 . benkyoo

47 . kyooshitsu

48 . shooboosho

49 . bijutsukan

50 . untenshu

付表1

ひらがなの字源　The Derivations of <u>Hiragana</u>.

あ 安	い 以	う 宇	え 衣	お 於
か 加	き 幾	く 久	け 計	こ 己
さ 左	し 之	す 寸	せ 世	そ 曽
た 太	ち 知	つ 川	て 天	と 止
な 奈	に 仁	ぬ 奴	ね 祢	の 乃
は 波	ひ 比	ふ 不	へ 部	ほ 保
ま 末	み 美	む 武	め 女	も 毛
や 也		ゆ 由		よ 与
ら 良	り 利	る 留	れ 礼	ろ 呂
わ 和	を 袁	ん 无		

— 52 —

第2部　　chart 2

か　た　か　な

1 課

ア a	イ i	ウ u	エ e	オ o
カ ka	キ ki	ク ku	ケ ke	コ ko
サ sa	シ shi	ス su	セ se	ソ so
タ ta	チ chi	ツ tsu	テ te	ト to
ナ na	ニ ni	ヌ nu	ネ ne	ノ no
ハ ha	ヒ hi	フ fu	ヘ he	ホ ho
マ ma	ミ mi	ム mu	メ me	モ mo
ヤ ya		ユ yu		ヨ yo
ラ ra	リ ri	ル ru	レ re	ロ ro
ワ wa	ン n			

ア	ア	ア	ア	ア				
イ	イ	イ	イ	イ				
ウ	ウ	ウ	ウ	ウ				
エ	エ	エ	エ	エ				
オ	オ	オ	オ	オ				
カ	カ	カ	カ	カ				
キ	キ	キ	キ	キ				
ク	ク	ク	ク	ク				
ケ	ケ	ケ	ケ	ケ				
コ	コ	コ	コ	コ				
サ	サ	サ	サ	サ				
シ	シ	シ	シ	シ				
ス	ス	ス	ス	ス				
セ	セ	セ	セ	セ				
ソ	ソ	ソ	ソ	ソ				

タ	ク ノ タ	タ	タ	タ				
チ	ニ 一 チ	チ	チ	チ				
ツ	゛ ゛ ツ	ツ	ツ	ツ				
テ	ニ 一 テ	テ	テ	テ				
ト	｜ ト	ト	ト	ト				
ナ	一 ナ	ナ	ナ	ナ				
ニ	一 ニ	二	二	二				
ヌ	フ ヌ	ヌ	ヌ	ヌ				
ネ	゛ ラ ネ	ネ	ネ	ネ				
ノ	ノ	ノ	ノ	ノ				
ハ	ノ ハ	ハ	ハ	ハ				
ヒ	一 ヒ	ヒ	ヒ	ヒ				
フ	フ	フ	フ	フ				
ヘ	ヘ	ヘ	ヘ	ヘ				
ホ	一 オ ナ ホ	ホ	ホ	ホ				

マ	マ	マ	マ	マ				
ミ	ミ	ミ	ミ	ミ				
ム	ム	ム	ム	ム				
メ	メ	メ	メ	メ				
モ	モ	モ	モ	モ				
ヤ	ヤ	ヤ	ヤ	ヤ				
ユ	ユ	ユ	ユ	ユ				
ヨ	ヨ	ヨ	ヨ	ヨ				
ラ	ラ	ラ	ラ	ラ				
リ	リ	リ	リ	リ				
ル	ル	ル	ル	ル				
レ	レ	レ	レ	レ				
ロ	ロ	ロ	ロ	ロ				
ワ	ワ	ワ	ワ	ワ				
ン	ン	ン	ン	ン				

2 課

ガ ga	ギ gi	グ gu	ゲ ge	ゴ go
ザ za	ジ ji	ズ zu	ゼ ze	ゾ zo
ダ da			デ de	ド do
バ ba	ビ bi	ブ bu	ベ be	ボ bo
パ pa	ピ pi	プ pu	ペ pe	ポ po

ガ								
ギ								
グ								
ゲ								
ゴ								
ザ								
ジ								
ズ								

ゼ ゾ ダ デ ド バ ビ ブ ベ ボ パ ピ プ ペ ポ

3 課

キャ kya	キュ kyu		キョ kyo
シャ sha	シュ shu	シェ she	ショ sho
チャ cha	チュ chu	チェ che	チョ cho
ニャ nya	ニュ nyu		ニョ nyo
ヒャ hya	ヒュ hyu		ヒョ hyo
ミャ mya	ミュ myu		ミョ myo
リャ rya	リュ ryu		リョ ryo
ギャ gya	ギュ gyu		ギョ gyo
ジャ ja	ジュ ju	ジェ je	ジョ jo
ビャ bya	ビュ byu		ビョ byo
ピャ pya	ピュ pyu		ピョ pyo
	ウィ wi	ウェ we	ウォ wo
クァ kwa			
ツァ tsa		ツェ tse	ツォ tso
	ティ ti		
ファ fa	フィ fi	フェ fe	フォ fo
	ディ di	デュ du	
（ヴァ va	ヴィ vi	ヴ vu	ヴェ ve	ヴォ vo）

4 課

外来語の表記のしかた

　外国語の音をそのまま日本の文字に置きかえることはできない。日本語にない音韻については，その文字がない。したがって，そのまま外国語の発音に忠実に表記できるはずがないのである。日本語の音韻でとらえて，日本語としての発音をし，それを表記するのである。

　たとえば，次のような音韻は日本語にないので，（　　　）中のような表記をすることが多い。

　th→（サ，シ，ス，セ，ソで表す）

　ti →（チで表す。原音にひかれて，「ティ」で表すこともある）

　di→（ジで表す。原音にひかれて，「ディ」で表すこともある）

　外国人学習者にとってむずかしいと思われる表記法をいくつかにまとめて練習してみよう。

How to Write Words of Foreign Origin

The sounds of foreign languages can not be transliterated accurately in Japanese because written Japanese does not have symbols for sounds not contained in the spoken language. Thus the sounds of foreign words can not be represented faithfully in written Japanese. Such words are interpreted within the Japanese sound system and given Japanese pronunciation, which can then be written in kana.

For example, the following sounds are not contained in Japanese; they are frequently represented by such kana as the ones in parentheses:

th → (サ, シ, ス, セ, ソ)

ti → (チ; sometimes written ティ to approximate the original sound more closely)

di → (ジ; sometimes written ディ to approximate the original sound more closely)

The exercises which follow focus on a number of sounds which foreign learners find particularly troublesome to write.

1. CVCVのように並んでいるもの

Words having a CVCV pattern

ma	ni	a		ca	me	ra		co	i	n
マ	ニ	ア		カ	メ	ラ		コ	イ	ン

〔れんしゅう〕

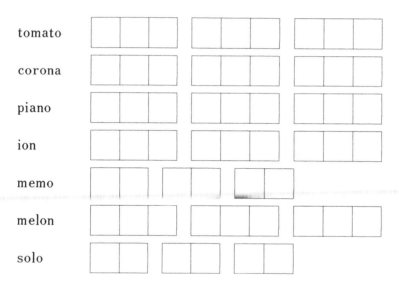

tomato

corona

piano

ion

memo

melon

solo

トマト　コロナ　ピアノ　イオン　メモ　メロン　ソロ

2.　—cc—のように子音が並んでいるときは，子音の後に適当な母音を添えて発音したり，表記したりする。

Words containing two or more consonant sounds in succession (—cc—) are pronounced and written with appropriate vowels placed after each consonant sound.

2-(1)　t, dには母音 o を添える。

t and d are followed by <u>o</u>.

hint → hinto　　ヒント
（ただし，salad はサラダと書く）
（exception:　salad becomes <u>sarada</u>, サラダ）

2-(2)　c，b，f，g，k，l，m，p，s には母音 u を添える。

c, b, f, g, k, l, m, p and a are followed by <u>u</u>.

mask → masuku　　マスク
post　→ posuto　　ポスト
milk　→ miruku　　ミルク

〔れんしゅう〕

swan								
test								
golf								
delta								

soft

emerald

coil

list

cent

sect

instant

oriental

esperanto

スワン　テスト　ゴルフ　デルタ　ソフト　エメラルド　コイル
リスト　セント　セクト　インスタント　オリエンタル　エスペラント

　なお，語末の—te のように，t や d に e がついても，2-(1) —t, —d と同じように，
ト・ドとなる。

Final —te and —de are handled in the same way as —t and —d, becoming
to(ト) and do(ド).

　　cf.　　note　ノート　　shade　シェード

また，語末のc，b，f，k，l，m，p，sにeがついても，2-(2)のように—uを添えた形になる。

When the original word ends in c, b, f, k, l, m, p or s followed by silent e, the consonant sound is followed by u in Japanese.

cf.　　simple　シンプル　　single　シングル　　knife　ナイフ
　　　　game　ゲーム　　grape　グレープ
　　　（ただし，—geのばあいは，ジになる）
　　　（However, —ge becomes ji, ジ.)

3. 長音の場合は「ー」をつけて表す。「ー」も1拍の長さとして発音しなければならない。

Long sounds are represented by a dash, ー. This dash indicates that the preceding vowel is given a duration of two moras.

よこ書きの場合（writing horizontally）　たて書きの場合（writing vertically）

seesaw	シ	ー	ソ	ー

queen	ク	イ	ー	ン

seesaw
シ
ー
ソ
ー

queen
ク
イ
ー
ン

3-(1) ーar, ーer ーir, ーur, ーor

car	カー	turban	ターバン
bar	バー	curtain	カーテン
garden	ガーデン	port	ポート
lever	レバー	form	フォーム
lover	ラバー	record	レコード
tanker	タンカー		
sir	サー		

語末のーorはオ列長音でなくア列長音になる。
Final ーor is expressed with a long ーaー sound, not a long ーoー sound.

skirt	スカート	sailor	セーラー
girl	ガール	doctor	ドクター
turn	ターン	error	エラー

カー　　バー　　ガーデン　　レバー　　ラバー　　タンカー　　サー

スカート　　ガール　　ターン　　ターバン　　カーテン　　ポート

フォーム　　レコード　　セーラー　　ドクター　　エラー

〔れんしゅう〕

harp

mark

Derby

river

bird

circle

sports

pork

hurdle

curl

doctor

motor

tailor

percent

concert

ハープ　　マーク　　ダービー　　リバー　　バード
サークル　　スポーツ　　ポーク　　ハードル　　カール
ドクター　　モーター　　テーラー　　パーセント　　コンサート

3-(2) —ee—, —ea—, —ai—, —oa—, —ou—, —au—, —oo—

speed	スピード	coupon	クーポン
cheese	チーズ	sauce	ソース
jeep	ジープ	auction	オークション
speech	スピーチ	audition	オーディション
seal	シール	overhaul	オーバーホール
pearl	パール	spoon	スプーン
rail	レール	room	ルーム
chain	チェーン	pool	プール
tail	テール		
road	ロード		
boat	ボート		
coat	コート		
group	グループ		

（—oo—，—ea—のあるものは促音の表記をすることがある）

(Some words spelled with —oo— and
—ea— are rendered in Japanese with a
double consonant sound. Cf. p.86.)

スピード　チーズ　ジープ　スピーチ　シール　パール
レール　チェーン　テール　ロード　ボート　コート
グループ　クーポン　ソース　オークション　オーディション
オーバーホール　スプーン　ルーム　プール

〔れんしゅう〕

beef

screen

queen

teak

leader

heart

rehearsal

cream

sausage

training

sailor

goal

broach

soap

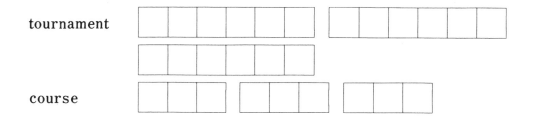

tournament

course

ビーフ　　スクリーン　　クイーン　　チーク　　リーダー　　ハート
リハーサル　　クリーム　　ソーセージ　　トレーニング　　セーラー
ゴール　　ブローチ　　ソープ　　トーナメント　　コース

3-(3)　—all,　—al,　—ol

call　コール　　　　　chalk　チョーク

ball　ボール　　　　　half　ハーフ

all　オール　　　　　old　オールド

balk　ボーク　　　　　gold　ゴールド

コール　　ボール　　オール　　ボーク　　チョーク　　ハーフ
オールド　　ゴールド

〔れんしゅう〕

roller												
squall												
folk												
talkie												
recall												
all												

ローラー　　スコール　　フォーク　　トーキー　　リコール　　オール

3-(4)　—w，—y

show	ショー	copy	コピー
screw	スクリュー	melody	メロディー
news	ニュース	salary	サラリー
ruby	ルビー	May Day	メーデー

ショー　　スクリュー　　ニュース　　ルビー　　コピー　　メロディー
サラリー　　メーデー

[れんしゅう]

straw

trawl

owner

whisky

party

elegy

authority

ストロー　　トロール　　オーナー　　ウイスキー　　パーティー

エレジー　　オーソリティー

3-(5)　—a—e, —o—e, —u—e

ace	エース	case	ケース
lace	レース	base	ベース
game	ゲーム	image	イメージ
name	ネーム	stage	ステージ

sale	セール	rope	ロープ
date	デート	isotope	アイソトープ
skate	スケート	stroke	ストローク
trade	トレード	dome	ドーム
parade	パレード	zone	ゾーン
arcade	アーケード	tone	トーン
note	ノート	nude	ヌード
hole	ホール	tube	チューブ

エース　　レース　　ゲーム　　ネーム　　ケース　　ベース

イメージ　　ステージ　　セール　　デート　　スケート　　トレード

パレード　　アーケード　　ノート　　ホール　　ロープ　　アイソトープ

ストローク　　ドーム　　ゾーン　　トーン　　ヌード　　チューブ

〔れんしゅう〕

base

space

rate

wave

brake

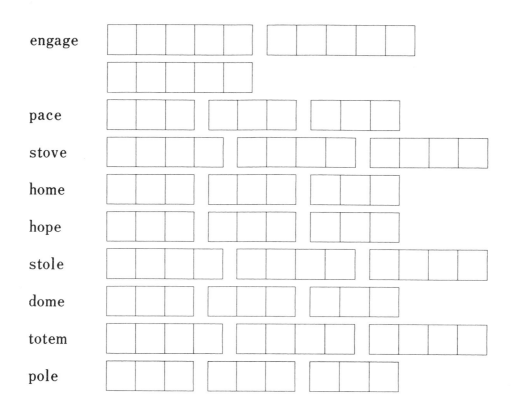

engage

pace

stove

home

hope

stole

dome

totem

pole

ベース　　スペース　　レート　　ウエーブ　　ブレーキ　　エンゲージ

ペース　　ストーブ　　ホーム　　ホープ　　ストール　　ドーム

トーテム　　ポール

3-(6)　—ation,　—otion

inflation　　インフレーション　　　　　　lotion　　ローション

inspiration　　インスピレーション　　　　motion　　モーション

intonation　　イントネーション

automation　　オートメーション

インフレーション　　インスピレーション　　イントネーション
オートメーション　　ローション　　モーション

3-(7)　—ire,　—ture

hire	ハイヤー	culture	カルチャー
fire	ファイヤー	adventure	アドベンチャー

ハイヤー　　ファイヤー　　カルチャー　　アドベンチャー

〔れんしゅう〕

dictation

deflation

decoration

narration

motion

umpire

picture

ディクテーション　　デフレーション　　デコレーション　　ナレーション
モーション　　アンパイヤー　　ピクチャー

4. つまる音の場合は，小さい「ッ」を添えて書き表す。

Some consonant clusters are represented by using small ッ.

4-(1) —ck

back	バック	block	ブロック
slacks	スラックス	trick	トリック
black	ブラック	check	チェック
dock	ドック	neck	ネック
socks	ソックス		

ただし，下のことばは，ckを促音化しない。うしろの部分が促音化する。

However, in the following words the final consonant is doubled rather than the medial —ck sound.

rocket　ロケット（ロッケトではない）

pocket　ポケット　　racket　ラケット

また次のことばは促音化しない。

Moreover, the following words contain no double consonant sounds.

bucket　バケツ　　necktie　ネクタイ

バ̚ック　　スラ̚ックス　　ブラ̚ック　　ド̚ック　　ソ̚ックス　　ブロ̚ック

ト̚リック　　チェ̚ック　　ネ̚ック

〔れんしゅう〕

truck			
snack			
lucky			
nickel			
check			
locker			
tuck			
socker			
racket			
ticket			

トラック　　スナック　　ラッキー　　ニッケル　　チェック

ロッカー　　タック　　サッカー　　ラケット　　チケット

4-(2)　—x, —tch, —dge

tax	タックス		match	マッチ
wax	ワックス		sketch	スケッチ
six	シックス		watch	ウォッチ
complex	コンプレックス		badge	バッジ

dodgeball　ドッジボール　　　　　　　edge　エッジ

タックス　　ワックス　　シックス　　コンプレックス　　マッチ
スケッチ　　ウォッチ　　バッジ　　エッジ　　ドッジボール

〔れんしゅう〕

box

sex

fox

deluxe

mix

scotch

hatch

catch

clutch

switch

bridge

badge ☐☐☐ ☐☐☐☐ ☐☐☐

ボックス　セックス　フォックス　デラックス　ミックス
スコッチ　ハッチ　キャッチ　クラッチ　スイッチ
ブリッジ　バッジ

4-(3)　—ss,　—pp,　—tt,　—ff

massage	マッサージ	slipper	スリッパ
message	メッセージ	motto	モットー
apple	アップル	marionette	マリオネット
pineapple	パイナップル	staff	スタッフ

—ss—,　—tt,　—pp—,　—ff—でも促音化しないものがある。

For some words containing —ss—, —tt—, —pp— and —ff—, the consonant sound is not doubled in Japanese.

語尾の—ssは促音化しない。

Final —ss is not doubled.

dress ドレス, chess チェス, pass パス, kiss キス, Miss ミス, など。

次のものも促音にならない。

The following are not given a double consonant sound:

butter　バター　appeal　アピール（アッピールとも書く　Also written アッピール）　approach　アプローチ　coffee　コーヒー
assistant　アシスタント　attraction　アトラクション

マッサージ　メッセージ　アップル　パイナップル
スリッパ　モットー　マリオネット　スタッフ

〔れんしゅう〕

mission

essay

dressy

essence

zipper

wappen(Ger.)

mitt

etiquette

address

chess

class

4-(4)　—at, —ap, —et, —ep, —ip, —op, —og, —ic, —ot,
　　　　etc…

mat	マット		ship	シップ
cat	キャット		skip	スキップ
net	ネット		drop	ドロップ
pet	ペット		bag	バッグ
omit	オミット		smog	スモッグ
cut	カット		magic	マジック
pilot	パイロット		technic	テクニック
cap	キャップ		olympic	オリンピック
			dynamic	ダイナミック

〔れんしゅう〕

rat

hat

jet

toilet

pot

robot

snap

overlap

tip

hip

top

dog

frog

picnic

italic

pacific

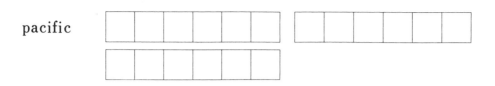

ラット　　ハット　　ジェット　　トイレット　　ポット　　ロボット

スナップ　　オーバーラップ　　チップ　　ヒップ　　トップ　　ドッグ

フロッグ　　ピクニック　　イタリック　　パシフィック

4-(5)　母音がかさなる場合（長音にならないで, 促音になる場合）

Words which are spelled with two vowels in a row but are rendered in Japanese with a double consonant sound rather than with a lengthened vowel sound.

—oo—,　—ea—,　—ou—,　—ui—

book	ブック	head	ヘッド
look	ルック	touch	タッチ
football	フットボール	couple	カップル
cookie	クッキー	circuit	サーキット
deadball	デッドボール	biscuit	ビスケット
bread	ブレッド		

ブック　　ルック　　フットボール　　クッキー　　デッドボール

ブレッド　　ヘッド　　タッチ　　カップル　　サーキット

ビスケット

〔れんしゅう〕

hook

foot

dead heat

bread

couple

biscuit

フック　　フット　　デッドヒート　　ブレッド
カップル　　ビスケット

付表 2

かたかなの字源　The Derivations of <u>Katakana</u>.

ア阿	イ伊	ウ宇	エ江	オ於
カ加	キ幾	ク久	ケ介	コ己
サ散	シ之	ス須	セ世	ソ曽
タ多	チ千	ツ川	テ天	ト止
ナ奈	ニ二	ヌ奴	ネ祢	ノ乃
ハ八	ヒ比	フ不	ヘ部	ホ保
マ末	ミ三	ム牟	メ女	モ毛
ヤ也		ユ由		ヨ与
ラ良	リ利	ル流	レ礼	ロ呂
ワ和	ン尓			

日本語
かな入門

英語版

○執筆　　河原崎　幹夫
　　　　　東京外国語大学附属日本語学校教授

○英文翻訳　バーバラ　杉原

○録音テープ

○監修　　河原崎　幹夫

○ナレーター　土岐　哲
　　　　　アメリカ・カナダ十一大学連
　　　　　合日本研究センター専任講師

□企画・編集　国際交流基金　日本語国際センター

○さし絵　　ジャック・ボックス

○表紙作品　十時　恵
○表紙レイアウト　ジャック・ボックス

NIHONGO:
KANA —AN INTRODUCTION TO THE
JAPANESE SYLLABARY

○Writing: Mikio Kawarazaki
           Professor, The Japanese Language School Attached
           to the Department of Foreign Language, Tokyo
           University of Foreign Studies

○English Translation: Barbara Sugihara

○Tape Recording

○Supervision: Mikio Kawarazaki

○Narration: Satoshi Toki
           Instructor, Inter-University Center for
           Japanese Language Studies

☐Planning and Editing: THE JAPAN FOUNDATION JAPANESE LANGUAGE INSTITUTE

○Illustrations: THE JACK BOX

○Cover Design
○Artist: Megumi Totoki
○Layout: THE JACK BOX

日本語　かな入門　英語版（新装版）

1978年　3月31日　第1版　第1刷発行
1981年　4月15日　第2版　第1刷発行
1983年　4月15日　第3版　第1刷発行
2023年11月30日　新装版　第1刷発行

著作権者　国 際 交 流 基 金
　　　　　〒160-0004　東京都新宿区四谷1-6-4
　　　　　　　　　　　四谷クルーセ1〜3階

　　　　　連絡先
　　　　　国 際 交 流 基 金
　　　　　日本語国際センター　教材開発チーム
　　　　　https://www.jpf.go.jp/urawa
　　　　　〒330-0074　埼玉県さいたま市浦和区北浦和5-6-36
　　　　　　　　　　　電話　048(834)1183

発　　行　株式会社 凡 人 社
　　　　　〒102-0093　東京都千代田区平河町1-3-13
　　　　　　　　　　　電話　03(3263)3959

ISBN 978-4-86746-020-7